Inside
Nordic Homes

INSPIRING SCANDINAVIAN LIVING

Agata Toromanoff

Inside
Nordic Homes
INSPIRING SCANDINAVIAN LIVING

BRAUN

Contents

006   Preface

008   Åstrup Have House

012   Archipelago House

018   Villa Aa

024   Villa E

028   Lauesen House

032   Blå Hus

038   Villa Ryysyranta II

042   Wave House

046   Matchbox Houses

050   House J

056   3-Square House

060   Cabin Rones

066   Dogs & Doctors House

072   Nisser Micro Cabin

076	House on an Island	148	Mylla Cabin
082	Bay Window House	154	Zieglers Nest
086	House in Bergen	160	Cabin in Ulvik
092	Brickhouse with Tower	164	Kvitfjell Cabin
096	Villa Hedberg	170	Kyvik House
102	Timraron 1118 Cabin	174	ABC Street House
108	Villa Vassdal	178	Villa Hovås
114	Petry Retreat	184	Villa MSV
118	L.A. Villa	190	Summerhouse T
122	David's Apartment	194	Hidden Tints
126	Vester Voldgade Apart.	200	Gummi's 40sqm Apart.
130	Bolig DoB House	204	Villa Bülowsvej
134	Risalleen House	208	Hytte Hvaler
138	Villa Berg	212	Shutter House
142	Skigard Hytte	218	Hlöðuberg Artist's Studio

Preface

Nordic architecture and interior design have for decades set the tone for innovation and trends that are then adopted worldwide. While the holistic principles that guide interior design in Scandinavia, and give them that unmistakable touch of harmony and comfort, are well known - such as the importance, given to the surrounding landscape, the essential role of light, the fluidity of spaces – individual houses envisioned by Nordic architects never cease to surprise and inspire us. Each time, the feeling is that the exterior look of the house and the interior spaces are in perfect concordance with the location, as if the building had captured the organic spirit of the place. The fact that Nordic architecture often draws on the wisdom of centuries-long, vernacular architecture to find modern solutions certainly contributes to this experience. Floor-to-ceiling windows, a frequent feature of common spaces, not only invites to contemplate the nature around, but also lets the light through the house, adding an aerial feeling even at the ground level. The fireplace, a source of light and warmth, provides a sense of intimate well-being that transforms interiors, in the heart of winter, into protective nests. The choice of materials is another essential component of interior design. Architects and designers seem to particularly care about blending various materials and contrasting textures, thus adding an original and cheerful note to the spaces. Pure, geometric lines are omnipresent, but they are in no way synonymous with coldness or monotony: their apparent simplicity adapts very well to complex, dynamic volumes and their proportions, which are always carefully thought out, are intended to offer some visual rest to our brain and a feeling of protective solidity, thus bringing their share to the cozy Nordic lifestyle.

All interiors featured in this book, in their great diversity, exemplify these concepts. Houses located in residential areas are shown next to lakeside cabins or summer houses hidden in the forest. They constitute a vibrant, and fascinating panorama of the Nordic lifestyle in the most recent years and reflect the quest for deep harmony with nature and the surrounding landscape, an approach that is undoubtedly the key to true sustainability. The aesthetic perfection of some buildings almost overshadows the complexity of the plot on which they are built and the challenges faced by the architects in balancing the houses' functionality, its simplicity of form, and its blending into the landscape. One can only admire the exceptional creativity of Nordic architects and interior designers and their ability to design spaces with a soul.

Page 2
Dogs & Doctors House
Pirinen & Salo Oy
Pyhtää, Finland / 2021
photography Marc Goodwin

Page 6
House on an Island
Atelier Oslo
Skåtøy Island, Norway / 2018
photography Ivar Kvaal

Architects: NORRØN Architects

Location: Haderslev, Denmark
Completion: 2020
Gross floor area: 600 m²
Photography: Torben Eskerod

Åstrup Have House

The silhouette of the house is a celebration of geometry with a sophisticated play between the wooden interiors and concrete outer wall.

NORRØN Architects designed a visually striking recreational residence echoing the region's traditional vernacular architecture. An ultra-contemporary incarnation of the traditional Danish farmhouse, Åstrup Have has been arranged around a central patio. Each wing has a different function: residential quarters, with culinary facilities opposite, the guest area, and a garage with a workshop. Thanks to numerous floor-to-ceiling windows, the residents can enjoy the scenic view of the Haderslev Fjord and the house's remote location. The interiors are thus filled with natural light. The architects selected an extraordinary range of materials with rich and often contrasting textures. While the structure is made of raw concrete, partly smooth and partly grooved, the grey façade is complemented by the details made of brass, but also by the thatched roof. Inside, the generous use of wood creates a cozy atmosphere but also enhances the sculptural and complex spaces. The house is a refined combination of raw, natural, contemporary, and traditional.

Architect: Norm Architects

Location: Sweden
Completion: 2020
Gross floor area: 124 m^2
Photography: Jonas Bjerre-Poulsen

Archipelago House

Set in a beautiful location on the Swedish coast, this summer holiday home is in perfect harmony with its unspoiled surroundings.

Drawing from local architectural traditions, the Norm Architects studio has designed four interlocking volumes as a contemporary interpretation of traditional boathouses occupying the rocky cliffs. Protectively embracing the wooden terrace and connected by a system of steps inside, all parts of the house follow the sloping terrain. The bright wooden outer shell blends the house into the natural context. Clean lines, bright spaces, and light hues define the interiors, which span five different levels. The relaxing design of all spaces is thanks to a well-balanced combination of natural materials, a muted color palette, and the exquisitely finished furniture celebrating craftsmanship. Last but not least, numerous large openings, even in the roof, allow residents to enjoy the beautiful scenery as well as natural light, and thus smooth the inside–outside relation, just like the careful and symbolic choice of colors and textures.

Architects: C.F. Møller Architects

Location: Vestfold, Denmark
Completion: 2019
Gross floor area: 375 m²
Photography: Ivar Kvaal

Villa Aa

Villa Aa, envisioned as a residence for the next generation of the family owning the farm, has been smoothly incorporated into the terrain. Part of the camouflage is a green rooftop that can be used as a terrace. The residence evolves as the terrain descends, with two water features and a pool on the lower terrace creating lovely mirrors for the sky to fuse the architecture with the surrounding nature. The architects minimized the impact on the surrounding area while complying with numerous regulations. Their modern element on the historical farm received two entrances – the main one leads to the spacious living area, which connects with a stunning view of the fjord through the entire glass façade. The second entrance, in the form of a small staircase with a green, bright courtyard, opens into space that is meant as an office, guest room, and fitness area. Concrete is the outer volume's main material, while it is wood that dominates the interiors.

A plot with a historic farm inhabited since the Viking Age in a protected part of the countryside near the Oslo Fjord welcomes an ultra-modern addition.

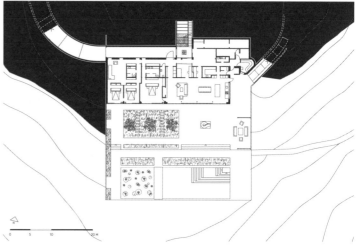

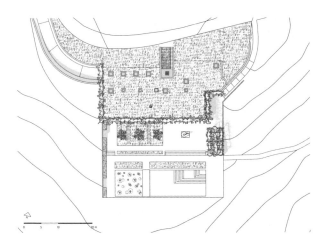

Architects: C.F. Møller Architects

Location: Risskov, Aarhus, Denmark
Completion: 2021
Gross floor area: 261 m^2
Photography: Julian Weyer

Villa E

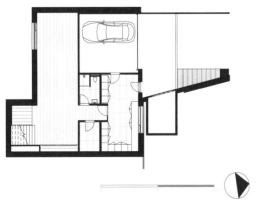

"Making the complex appear simple, elegant and timeless has been incredibly exciting and also a challenge", comments architect Klaus Toustrup, Partner at C.F. Møller Architects.

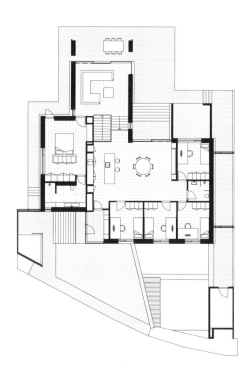

Villa E received a playful geometric volume made of four saddle roof elements and spread across two levels. The terraced structure was conceived due to the sloping character of the terrain in this residential district of Aarhus. C.F. Møller Architects based the concept, materials, and level of details on the iconic Aarhus University building, also designed by the studio. The rustic charm of the hand-painted bricks in shades of red that are used for the façade and roofs gives the house a compact outer shell, which is balanced by the large glazing on the garden façade that fills the rooms with natural light. Oak features visually reduce the inside–outside division. The interiors are also connected in a flowing manner. The heart of the house is a large kitchen and family room with a striking curved ceiling and access to the garden and to the four children's rooms. A couple of steps down is the living room section with an entrance to the parents' bedroom and the outdoor terrace.

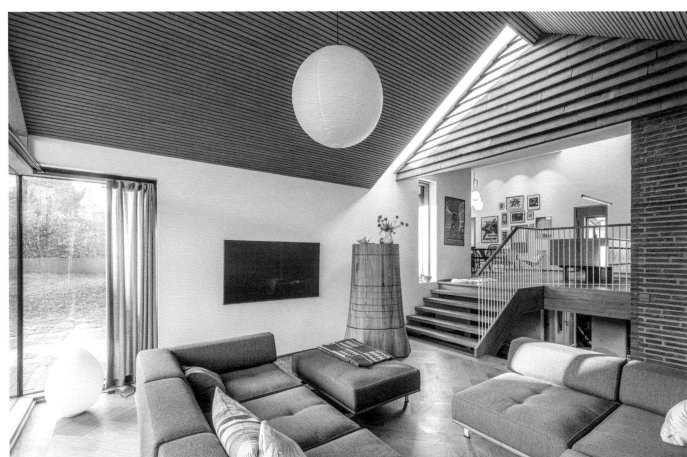

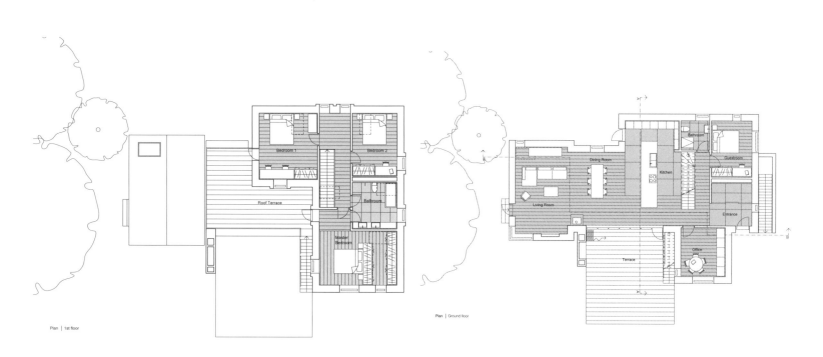

Plan | 1st floor

Plan | Ground floor

The meticulous brickwork façades
and brick-clad roofs evoke the style
of a traditional English cottage that is
combined with Scandinavian simplicity.

Architects: Sigurd Larsen Design & Architecture

Location: Roskilde, Denmark
Completion: 2020
Gross floor area: 172 m²
Photography: Tia Borgsmidt

Blå Hus

Two children's rooms have a particular character – one features a horizontal panoramic window along the desk, the other has a loft bed with a small opening at the highest point of the house.

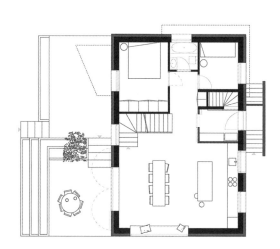

Blå Hus – the blue monolithic house – has a corrugated steel façade and roof that blend the volume with the hues of the Scandinavian sky, or that turn it into an optimistic element on rainy days. Sitting on a small hill, the house has been envisioned as a tall, narrow form to offer glimpses of the fjord as well as the medieval center of Roskilde. With numerous irregularly placed openings to frame the views on various sides, the cube creates a simple yet distinctive addition to the landscape. The arrangement of the main living space is spread over two levels with an open kitchen and dining room on the mid floor. A large terrace connects this part with the garden. Located in the upper part, the spacious living room is certainly the highlight of the interiors. A generous large corner window opens onto both the city's cathedral and the fjord and is a great spot for enjoying picturesque sunsets.

Architect: PAVE Architects

Location: Finland
Completion: 2017
Gross floor area: 160 m²
Photography: Arno de la Chapelle

Villa Ryysyranta II

Blending into the landscape of the Finnish island of Hailuoto, Villa Ryysyranta II is an evolution of an earlier design. The architects were able to subtly fuse it into the vegetation, which remains mainly untouched, by the use of specially treated larch in a grey tone. The inhabitants can enjoy the outdoors not only during the summer, on generously sized terrace areas, but also all year long thanks to the large glass openings that become a screen opening to the surrounding nature, changing together with the seasons. The villa's interiors, also made of larch wood throughout, are spread across three overlapping levels adjusted to the unique terrain. The ground floor is occupied by separately placed bedrooms, and the second floor has the main entrance as well as a lounge area that rises half a level above the plot for the best views of the beach and ocean. There is also a spacious sleeping loft, making the most of the volume's height. Both the placement of the volumes and their small scale reduce the visual impact of the villa on the landscape.

The architects' goal was
a delicate balance between
the pine wood of the beach
landscape and traditional
contemporary architecture.

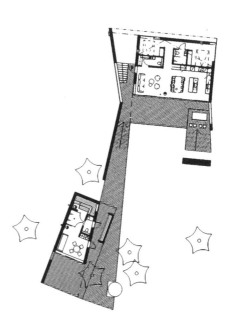

Architect: Seppo Mäntylä

Location: Mikkeli, Finland
Completion: 2017
Gross floor area: 300 m²
Photography: Hans Koistinen

Wave House

Inspired by the design of boats and airplanes, the striking, dynamic structure of Wave House is made of solid wood, glass, and steel.

As the architect observes, while curvaceous shapes are common in public buildings, using the shape in a single-family house is a challenging task. Seppo Mäntylä's Wave House is the result of a collaboration with Polar Life Haus, a renowned Finnish family company that specializes in high-quality wooden homes. The prototype, built in the spectacular lake environment in Mikkeli, Finland, demonstrates the prefab technique, which can be adjusted to the particular topography of a plot or owners' needs by enlarging the lower level. The general shape of the roof as well as the upper floor remain unchanged. Its walls are made of glass and of spruce logs. The dramatically shaped roof has been constructed from a combination of curved steel and wooden beams. Combined with this structure are ventilation and thermal insulation. While the architects selected felt as the outer roofing material, the roof's sidings are made of painted plywood elements. The glazed walls pull the lake views into the mainly open-plan interiors.

Architects: Avanto Architects

Location: Espoo, Finland
Completion: 2019
Gross floor area: 360 m²
Photography: Arsi Ikäheimonen

Matchbox Houses

Compared by the architects to block-like, overlapping matchboxes, two houses are perfectly incorporated into a gently sloping plot near the sea.

"The challenge was to solve two detached houses in place of one demolished house so that the buildings would naturally sit on the plot, providing both houses with privacy and the best views," comment Avanto Architects. Old stone fences, rocks, and pine trees have been preserved to create a special atmosphere outdoors. The inhabitants can enjoy the vast gardens as well as the covered terrace below the upper floor overhangs and the sunny roof terraces over the lower floor roof, with stunning views. Arranging the volumes this way was the key task for the architects, who used cast concrete for the frame of the buildings and long, low brick in various shades, enhanced by the play of sunlight, for the façade. The spacious interiors on both levels gain a lot of natural light through large openings and the glass-covered space connecting the two floors (with energy-efficient glazing). Geothermal heating and self-sufficient ground cooling systems make the houses self-regulating and eco-friendly buildings.

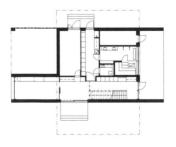

Architects: Avanto Architects

Location: Helsinki, Finland
Completion: 2021
Gross floor area: 456 m²
Photography: kuvio.com

House J

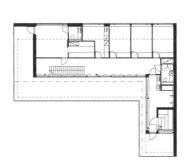

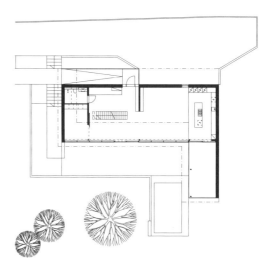

This rectangular volume, elegantly curved around an old pine tree, creates a private oasis with interiors entirely open to a sheltered courtyard with a pool.

House J, for a family of five, occupies the top of a high hill in a residential area of Helsinki. On one side it borders neighboring houses, on the other, it opens onto a forest. While the entrance façade is rather solid, the garden one has been entirely glazed to connect the interiors with the surrounding context. The windows on the ground floor provide direct access to the outdoor relaxation area (partly roofed), while the bedrooms on the upper level allow residents to enjoy views of the surrounding nature. While the height of the house is adjusted to that of the other buildings in the area, the top section is cantilevered, which together with the L-shape animates this sharp-edged, geometric form. From the open-plan lower level, an airy wooden staircase, suspended lightly in the air, leads to the second floor with the bedrooms. The concrete load-bearing walls are left exposed in contrast to the wooden window and door frames in natural oak.

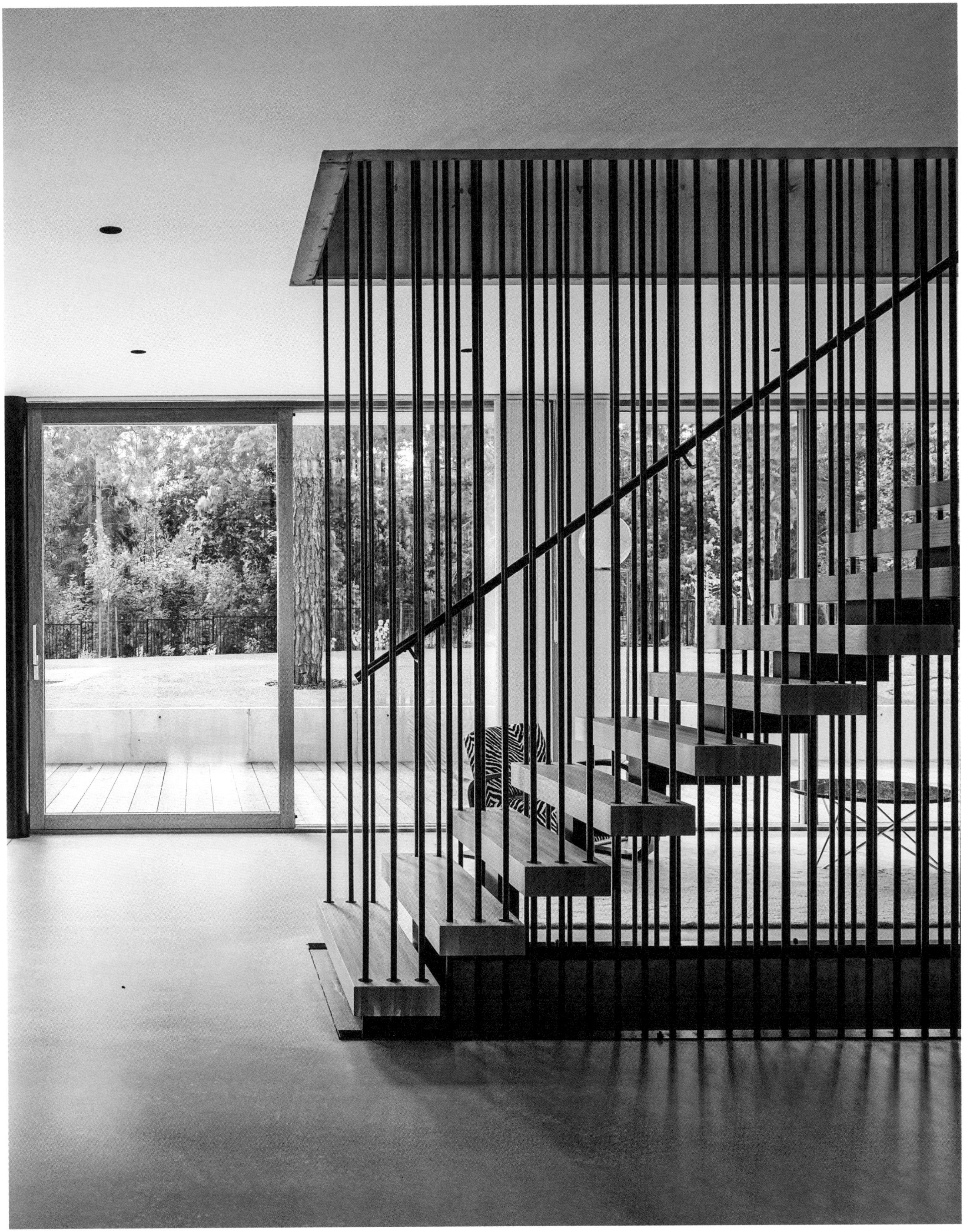

This multifaceted volume, surrounded by a dense spruce forest next to a lake, exemplifies a harmonious relationship between architecture and nature.

Architect: Studio Puisto

Location: Southern Savonia, Finland
Completion: 2019
Gross floor area: 165 m^2
Photography: Marc Goodwin, Archmospheres

3-Square House

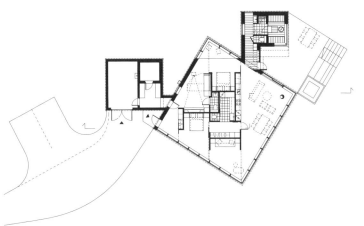

The location of the 3-Square House was based on the views, and for its construction, only one maple tree on site had to be removed. On the side of the adjacent lake, the structure is higher than the terrain to create the impression of floating above the water, while the paving stones of the lower part of the house are meant to echo the stone embankment of the shore. Strikingly, the generously glazed walls bring the landscape into the interiors. The architects envisioned the residence in the form of three interlocking volumes, each with different functions. While the smaller ones include a sauna, utility facilities, a garage and technical facilities, the central volume contains the living, dining, and sleeping areas. This core is not divided traditionally into specific rooms, yet spaces can be separated from each other by sliding doors. The exterior is made of wood, glass, and sheet zinc, while the interiors are entirely dominated by various types of wood, which interact with the natural light to create a special atmosphere.

Architects: Sanden+Hodnekvam Architects

Location: Steinkjer, Norway
Completion: 2018
Gross floor area: 47 m^2
Photography: Sanden+Hodnekvam Architects

Cabin Rones

As an observation point,
Cabin Rones becomes part
of a steep slope, embracing
a panoramic vista of the fjord.

The cabin was designed as a compact building to reduce the intervention of architecture into the site as well as to preserve its vegetation.
A well-balanced combination of concrete and cross-laminated timber, the residence is two levels high with the lower one adapting to the terrain. With its protective concrete base, high chimney, and triangular top section made of cross-laminated timber wrapped in black roofing felt, the cabin becomes a curious yet not invasive addition to the landscape. The living area is entirely open to the view through the glass façade directed toward the fjord. The interior spaces, equipped with large wooden windows, are interconnected fluidly. The furnishings, made of Norwegian birch, are devoid of superfluous elements and work well with the raw concrete walls and polished concrete floor. The minimalist interior and its reduced color palette harmonize with the quietness of the natural surroundings. The architects succeeded in creating a sheltering atmosphere and enhancing the connection with the surrounding nature at the same time.

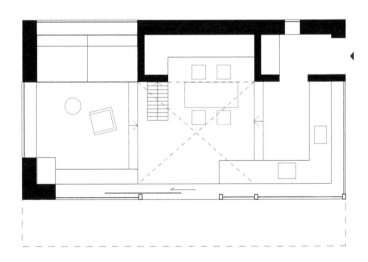

Architects: Pirinen & Salo Oy

Location: Pyhtää, Finland
Completion: 2021
Gross floor area: 220 m²
Photography: Marc Goodwin

Dogs & Doctors House

Dogs & Doctors House adjusts to its context like a chameleon –
its wooden base is topped with green pitched roofs imitating
the trees that surround it. The three separate volumes create
a spatial distribution that fits well into the surroundings without
dominating them. The architects' main goal was to provide plenty
of sea views, a feature that can be enjoyed from every room
of the house. The vistas of the archipelago form a part of the interiors.
This dramatic spatial experience is created through the ceiling height –
the entrance leads from a low hall to a spacious dining area with
a fireplace, which evolves into the living room, a few steps lower
with a spectacular opening looking out on the seashore. A massive
sliding door creates a passage to the coziest part of the house,
namely the main bedroom. With the all-wood walls and ceiling,
as well as the low windows, the interiors create the impression
of being in a treehouse, while the warmth and natural hue
of the wood create a special atmosphere.

Amid the pine trees of a Finnish coastline, these three pitched-roof volumes are visually intriguing thanks to their façades made of wood burned to char with a touch of vivid color.

Architect: Feste Landscape • Architecture

Location: Nissedal, Norway
Completion: 2017
Gross floor area: 26 m²
Photography: Smarte Hytter AS, David Fjågesund

Nisser Micro Cabin

Designed to be floating over a lake, Nisser Micro Cabin, with its natural charm, blends into nature and puts the inhabitants in the middle of it.

The design is a prototype of a micro cabin, originally envisioned
for a cabin developer as a floating one but placed on stilts due
to the local planning restrictions of Nisser lake in Norway. At the heart
of the concept was sustainability. While access to electricity, water,
and sewage is provided through a flexible pipe entering from underneath
the cabin, the gutters and downpipes are integrated into the external
walls. This creates clean walls, which, like the roof, are clad in thermally
treated pinewood. The natural outer shell also blends the house into
the landscape. Despite the small floor size, significantly enlarged
by the mezzanine, the cabin can accommodate up to seven people.
"The design attempts to maximize the user's experience of the lake
and the surrounding landscape," state the architects. A massive roofed
outdoor terrace links the panorama with the interiors. The glazed façade
welcomes natural light into the interconnected dining and living areas.

Architects: Atelier Oslo

Location: Skåtøy Island, Norway
Completion: 2018
Gross floor area: 70 m²
Photography: Ivar Kvaal

House
on an Island

This elegant summer house on the southern coast of an island in Norway was built for two artists as a place for contemplation and creative work.

The lightweight structure, made of meticulously interwoven wooden elements, sits gently on the rocky terrain. The curvatures of the rocks lead directly towards the ocean, while the house becomes an organic part of the coast, resembling a nest. The architects adjusted the various levels of the house to the topography to create numerous outdoor spaces. At the heart of the concept was also the goal of eliminating a clear outside–inside division. The house is designed to allow the residents to experience various aspects of the landscape when walking through the interiors. This connection is enhanced by the concrete floors which evoke the rocks below. The furnishings are reduced to the minimum and masterfully incorporated into the structure to leave the open space visually unobstructed. The timber structure is prefabricated and meant to direct the views and filter the natural light. The complex pattern of the walls create a play of shadows that recalls the experience of sitting under a tree on a sunny day.

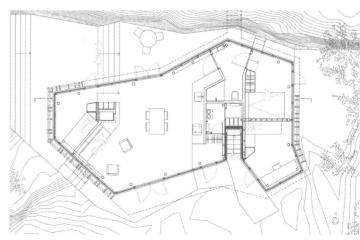

Architect: Atelier Oslo

Location: Mosjøen, Norway
Completion: 2020
Gross floor area: 600 m²
Photography: Kristoffer Wittrup

Bay Window House

The gigantic bay windows are the most striking feature of this multifaceted wooden volume, the complexity of which counter-balances the scale and creates separate outdoor spaces.

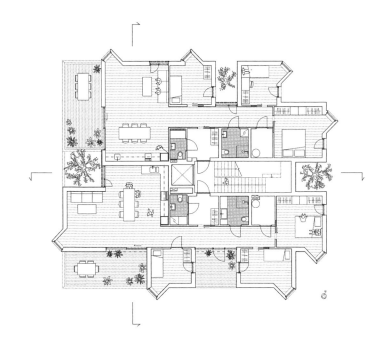

Located in Mosjøen, a town with a harbor close to the Lofoten Islands and residential areas characterized by a strict grid plan, this three-storey building houses four individual apartments. The design was envisioned for people who prefer an apartment rather than a single-family house with the architects' ambition to combine the simplicity of a flat with all the qualities of living in a house. The initially flat plot was reorganized to create an enriched topography with varied heights to diversify the way the building is connected with the ground and, together with newly planted vegetation, to provide privacy for the ground-floor apartment. The scale of the ground floor and second floor echoes that of the surrounding detached houses, while the first floor is larger and has been split into smaller volumes, which become canopies for the ground level and terraces for the top floor. The most distinctive element of each apartment are the full-height bay windows that are rhythmically rotated 45 degrees in relation to the building.

Architects: Kvalbein Korsøen Arkitektur

Location: Fana, Norway
Completion: 2019
Gross floor area: 130 m^2
Photography: Kvalbein Korsøen Arkitektur

House in Bergen

Built for a family with two small children, the house was designed based on two objectives. First, the architects aimed to create a perfect environment for childhood experiences, and second, nature was prioritized over architecture. "The two large maples on the site are the main premises for the size and shape of the house and the openings in the walls," remarks the studio. Based on a wooden frame structure that is filled with wood fiber insulation, the spaces of the house have been carefully planned. The tunnel-like, curved entrance leads to an airy open-space living area with a kitchen, which is connected to the garden. The upper floor, topped with a pitched roof, is divided into private bedrooms. The interiors on both levels are wrapped in pine cladding, which inspires a warm and pleasant atmosphere. The wood will darken over time in harmony with the natural surroundings.

The traditional materials, form, and building technique make this house a perfect, cozy nest for a perfect family life.

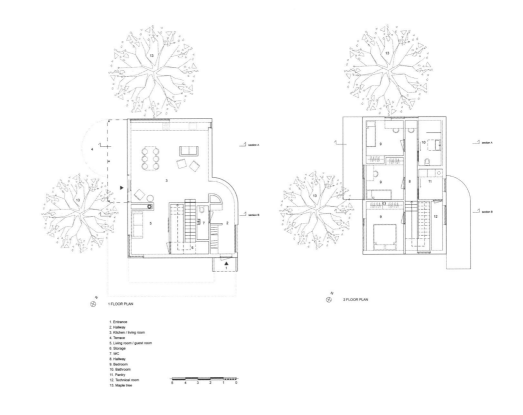

1 FLOOR PLAN

2 FLOOR PLAN

1. Entrance
2. Hallway
3. Kitchen / living room
4. Terrace
5. Living room / guest room
6. Storage
7. WC
8. Hallway
9. Bedroom
10. Bathroom
11. Pantry
12. Technical room
13. Maple tree

Architects: Sanden+Hodnekvam Architects

Location: Flugsrud, Lillehammer, Norway
Completion: 2022
Gross floor area: 220 m^2
Photography: Sanden+Hodnekvam Architects

Brickhouse with Tower

"Our interest was to find a way to build a brick house with a rational economy and an honesty in terms of tectonic qualities and a visible structure," state the architects. Brick was also selected due to its durability and timelessness. In addition, the long masonry traditions in the region led them to use traditional masonry techniques in the load-bearing construction. Both the volume and openings have been planned to avoid the excessive use of reinforcements like steel or concrete. The brick-wooden minimalist tower on a steep hill over-looks the lake of Mjøsa and the city center. The most striking elements of the interiors are the impressive roof beams in pine and ash plywood on the ceiling and ash plywood on the walls. While the tower, partly open to the floor below, functions as a kind of a library with extensive views, the main living space, with a kitchen and the bedrooms, is located on the first floor.

This voluminous house has a load-bearing wooden structure complemented by its distinctive cladding of coal-fired brick in various hues of red, which is also used as weather protection.

This compact summer house
for a family of four becomes
part of its picturesque landscape
of sand dunes planted with tall
pine trees.

Architects: Marge Arkitekter

Location: Åhus, Sweden
Completion: 2018
Gross floor area: 208 m²
Photography: Johan Fowelin

Villa Hedberg

Since the plot is part of a larger property, the new summer house was intended to be an oasis of privacy. The distinctive shape of the roof, the only element of the villa visible from the beach, is repeated in two smaller buildings – a sauna and a guest house. In between them, the inhabitants can enjoy a protected outdoor space. The architects included large wooden shutters, as the building's second skin, to allow the house to be entirely closed during the winter. When the shutters are open, and thus hidden, in the summer they reveal large glass panes in the façade, which have been placed to frame the coastal views, while the visual connection with neighboring buildings is reduced to a minimum. These two skins have been also differentiated through the use of two types of paneling – more conventional for the fixed elements and more rustic for the sliding parts – made of environmentally friendly pine that will weather with time to blend the architecture into the context.

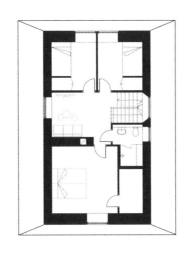

Architects: Ida Katrine Friis Tinning

Location: Sweden
Completion: 2018
Gross floor area: 90 m²
Photography: Ander Ingvartsen

Timraron 1118 Cabin

The combination of a quiet color palette and limited number of materials creates a comfortable open-space nest in the middle of nature.

Built on a slope between the sea and unspoiled woods, the Timraron Cabin is in harmony with nature. Thanks to many large openings on both façades, the inhabitants can enjoy striking views in two directions. Envisioned as a year-round residence, the villa, made of timber and glass, was placed on a concrete plinth. This intervention creates a visual illusion as if the house were partly levitating towards the seafront, and it also made it possible to reduce the impact on the plot and the existing nature. From the outset, it was the architecture being adapted to the environment and not the opposite. Blurring any boundaries between the inside and outside, the cabin is the architects' hide-out on Timraro island in the Stockholm archipelago. The common spaces as well as private rooms are wrapped in warm wooden paneling, while the interior design, in the Scandinavian spirit, is accompanied by many customized furnishing solutions that reduce waste by using spillover materials from construction.

Architects: Studio Holmberg

Location: Gothenburg, Sweden
Completion: 2019
Gross floor area: 120 m²
Photography: Marcus Bülow

Villa Vassdal

With façades and roofs shaped to match the exposed cliffs, the villa's monolithic form is clad in untreated heart-pine, which has been chosen to grey over time and become one with the rocky, natural background. The house "is imitating the characteristics and scale of the site with a low profile and broken up shifting volumes," as the architects remark. This spatial arrangement not only divides the functions but is also intended to create spaces that are both weather-protected and secluded. The layout of the interiors is planned not only to provide privacy from the neighbors and protection from excess light but also to open all rooms to the seascape. Another important goal for the architects was to create an indoor–outdoor relation in each space. The compact character of the volume is echoed by the walls and ceilings, all in birch plywood, inside. The box-like effect of the natural wood allows the inhabitants to enjoy contact with nature while being wrapped in a warm ambiance.

Set into the rocky, coastal landscape on a small island in the Gothenburg archipelago, the wooden volume of Villa Vassdal blends harmoniously into the surroundings.

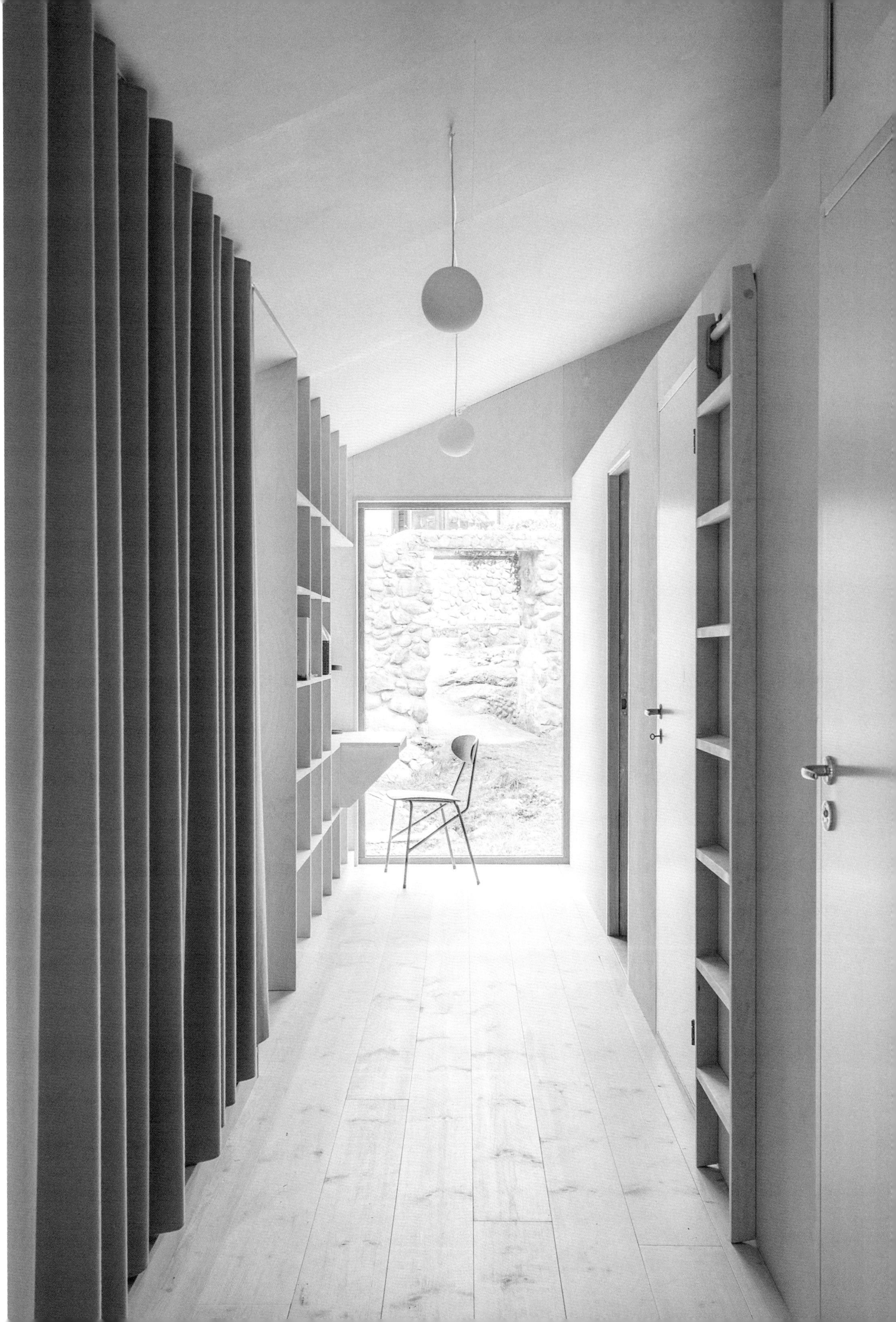

Architects: N+P ARKITEKTUR

Location: Denmark
Completion: 2018
Gross floor area: 120 m²
Photography: N+P ARKITEKTUR

Petry Retreat

Hidden in a scenic dune landscape thanks to its wooden structure and green roof, the Petry Retreat is perfectly tuned with the plot.

The wooden construction of the house is covered with thermo ash wood, and the pitched roof with sedum – both solutions act as a kind of camouflage. The dreamy setting of the plot, with a 180-degree panoramic view of the North Sea coastline, required an intimate design that would not spoil the existing nature. The well-balanced geometry of the volume also relates to nature. The floor plan offers a perfect balance between private and social spaces, with the former hidden conveniently from the wind on the side. The common living area, in contrast, is a spacious open space directed towards the sea. The mostly glazed walls, mainly made of sliding doors, create a direct connection with nature. Additionally, around the whole house, a large wooden terrace allows inhabitants to enjoy the outdoors from each room. Interestingly, just behind the house, there is a concrete bunker from the Second World War that the house's owners use for wine rooms and firewood.

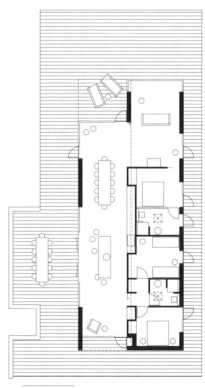

Architects: N+P Architecture

Location: Højbjerg, Denmark
Completion: 2017
Gross floor area: 340 m²
Photography: N+P Architecture

L.A. Villa

The geometric juxtaposition
of solid and empty creates
a playful effect in a very
minimalist volume.

The villa is located in a residential district in Højbjerg, near Århus, Denmark, that is characterized by its hilly terrain. The architects based the concept on a simple cube but played with the openings and outdoor spaces in an original way to create a dynamic inside–outside relation. In doing so, they turned the minimalist rectangle building into a curious volume with surprising cut-out elements, including flat windows and three-dimensional carved areas like terraces, both roofed and open. A system of stairs designed around the house provides smooth communication between two levels and the garden. Enhancing the shape is the role of the outer shell, made of bricks in a range of hues that glimmer in the sunlight throughout the day. The sharp edges and flat surfaces become lively and dynamic. Thanks to numerous windows and outdoor connections, as well as the open-space character, the interiors are spacious and bright. In addition to brick, the architects also used concrete, cedar wood, and copper.

Architect: David Thulstrup

Location: Copenhagen, Denmark
Completion: 2019
Gross floor area: 140 m²
Photography: Irina Boersma

David's Apartment

In the spirit of "modern simplicity",
a signature of David Thulstrup's style,
this atmospheric apartment demonstrates
the timeless charm of pared-down designs.

Known for his holistic approach to architecture and interiors as well as product design, the Danish designer David Thulstrup envisioned this 1920s apartment as his new home. Skillfully interweaving Scandinavian heritage with modern design language, the space is subtly lit and generously sized. The separated kitchen transforms through a dining area into a large living room, creating an L-shaped space that is free of superfluous elements. The carefully selected elements of furnishing form a comfortable, calm, and embracing environment. Most visually striking amid the general minimalist tone is a great sense of materiality and sophisticated combinations, both tactile and of colors. Light plays a special role in this effect: filtered through horizontal blinds, it interacts with various surfaces and hues of the interior. Light, color, and forms are all treated as architectural elements by the designer, who often creates custom pieces of furniture and lighting for a perfectly harmonious interplay of all elements of the interior and the architecture itself.

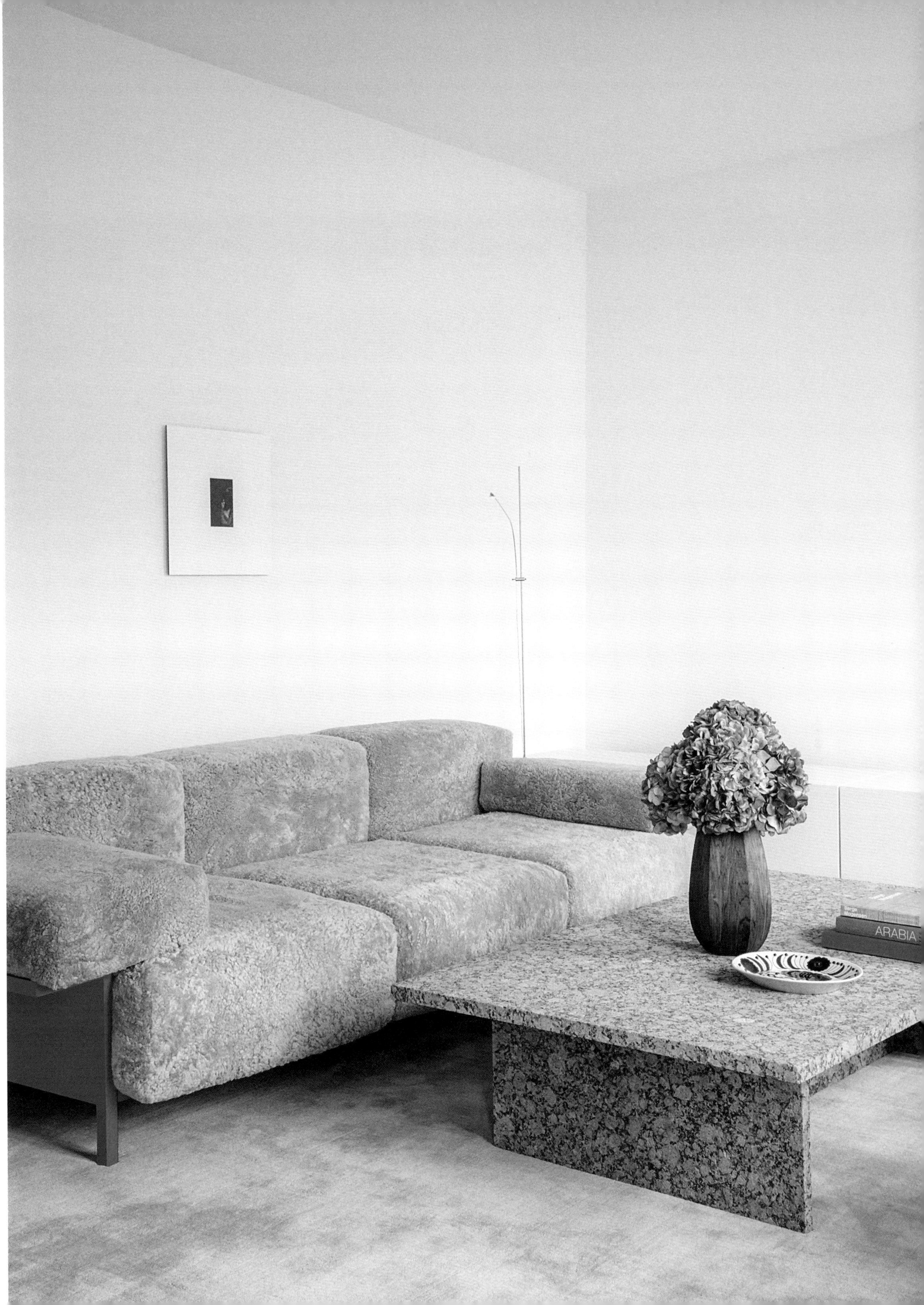
ARABIA

Architect: David Thulstrup

Location: Copenhagen, Denmark
Completion: 2020
Gross floor area: 150 m²
Photography: Irina Boersma

Vester Voldgade Apartment

The starting point was making this top floor apartment from the 1890s a bright living space with enlarged openings and outdoor terraces. The owners also wished to enhance the feeling of space. In the pursuit of both, David Thulstrup suggested a series of interventions. "By opening up the volumes of the living spaces both vertically and horizontally and using quality materials, I re-introduced a feeling of calmness and balance into a space that was marked by low ceilings and limited natural light," he comments. The acquisition of the attic space just above the flat enabled a fantastic double-height living space with access to the pitch roof structure. Pierced with openings, it invites even more sunlight inside. The neutral color palette is a perfect background for original elements of the structure, like the exposed old timber beams on both levels. Another connection between the two floors is a dramatically spiraled steel staircase, leading to a reading nook and the roof terrace with its panoramic vistas of the city.

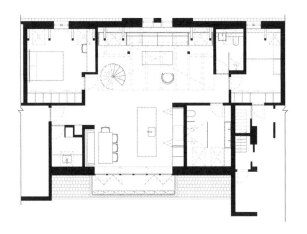

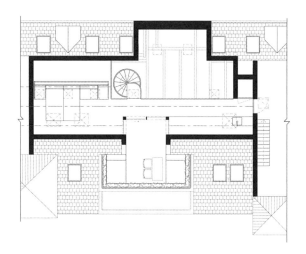

A warm and elegant combination of contemporary design and historic architecture results in an airy and spacious living space in a rooftop apartment in Copenhagen.

Architects: Lie Øyen arkitekter

Location: Nesodden, Norway
Completion: 2017
Gross floor area: 320 m^2
Photography: Jonas Adolfsen

Bolig DoB House

The L-shaped volume was designed in strong relation to the surrounding landscape – the shape of the roofs, as well as the ceilings, echo the lines of the terrain, while the geometric angle of the plan interacts with the steep hill nearby. The house not only envelops a sunny garden from the southwest but also opens the interiors to a striking view of the fjord and the city of Oslo to the north and east. To highlight the natural surroundings, large and randomly located openings introduce the lush nature into the warm and cozy interiors, which are dominated by wood. Envisioned on two levels in the form of multiple overlapping zones for the family to enjoy, the house has stairs as the central connecting element. The plan includes interlocking areas more than specific rooms to create common spaces for the whole family. "It is a house made for people, connections, and activities," note the architects.

This dynamically shaped building made of concrete, wood, and copper cladding reflects the irregularity of the terrain, while enveloping a quiet garden with a stunning view.

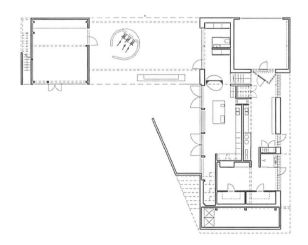

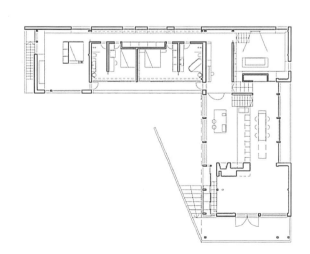

R21 Arkitekter completely reorganized the plot by renovating an existing house and integrating it with two new single-family houses on the site. One of the main references was the gabled roofs. Connected through a private garden that creates a common outdoor space, all houses have the same focus – the view and light. The lightweight construction combines natural wood and glass, which results in airy interiors, that smoothly communicated with the surrounding garden as well as with the neighboring houses. The space of Risalleen House has been divided into two levels, which are still visually connected – the lower floor has a large living area enlarged by an outdoor space, while the top part includes the kitchen and dining area. Continuous window strips of various heights enhance the dynamism of the double-height space. While the beech cladding defines the outer look, exposed wooden structures embrace the interiors to create a comfortable and warm atmosphere inside.

Architects: R21 Arkitekter

Location: Oslo, Norway
Completion: 2017
Gross floor area: 240 m²
Photography: Åke Eson Lindman

Risalleen House

The lightness and complexity of the timber structure is rustically highlighted by the vertical laminated wood cladding.

Architects: R21 Arkitekter

Location: Oslo, Norway
Completion: 2020
Gross floor area: 390 m²
Photography: Ruben Ratkusic

Villa Berg

Adjusted perfectly to the challenging conditions on the site, this villa is a curious composition of geometric forms, offering a complex yet intimate family home.

A mélange of the concrete base and brick top portions in a matching color palette makes the villa a sophisticated element of the landscape and another example of R21 Arkitekter's great sense of volumes. Sitting on a narrow plot in one of the residential areas of Oslo, it has been planned away from the road, which it faces with only a narrow and mainly blind façade. The shape follows the rhythm of the neighboring houses, while the prolonged volume is adjusted to the sloping character of the terrain. As such, despite the other residences around it, Villa Berg offers a connection with the garden space and ample privacy.

The architects planned encircling brick walls around the outdoor kitchen and terrace, as well as the pool, to provide even more intimacy for the inhabitants. This courtyard significantly enlarges the interiors on the first floor thanks to an entirely glazed wall, which is a source of natural light.

Architect: Mork-Ulnes Architects

Location: Norway
Completion: 2019
Gross floor area: 145 m^2
Photography: Bruce Damonte

Skigard Hytte

Situated nearly one thousand meters above sea level with sweeping views of a valley, the cabin was designed by architects Casper and Lexie Mork-Ulnes for their family. Their main decision was to detach the structure from the terrain to reduce the impact on the site to a minimum. A regular grid of 45 cross-laminated timber (CLT) wooden columns perched upon the steep hillside allows the grass to grow and sheep to walk freely around under the house. These columns are clad with skigard, a long and narrow quarter-cut tree log, traditionally laid out diagonally as fencing on Norwegian farms. The roof, overgrown with native grasses, is a reference to the traditional sod roofs that used to be common in rural Scandinavia. While the interior is planned as an enfilade of rooms with a central corridor, at the heart is the common living, dining, and kitchen area with 6-meter-long floor-to-ceiling glass walls inviting the landscape in. Three bedrooms, a sauna, and a guest annex complete the programme.

Every surface of the house is clad
in wood – outside this attunes
the cabin to the natural context,
and inside, smooth light pine
paneling creates an intimate feel.

Architects: Mork-Ulnes Architects

Location: Jevnaker, Norway
Completion: 2017
Gross floor area: 84 m²
Photography: Bruce Damonte

Mylla Cabin

Set in a scenic Norwegian forest, Mylla Cabin is made of untreated pine, weathering with time and fusing into the landscape.

Another family retreat in a remote location (yet only one hour away from Oslo), Mylla Cabin is a carefully planned response to the natural context. Standing on a hilltop with Mylla Lake below, the house was given a pinwheel structure not only to allow the owners to benefit from the different landscapes in all directions but also to separate the bedrooms for privacy. The complexity and dynamism of the form are enhanced by its gable roof, required by local regulations, which here was split in half to create a roof for each of the four volumes. This original arrangement is also a functional solution, as it creates two outdoor areas sheltered from the wind and snow. The efficiently planned interiors include three bedrooms, two bathrooms and a small annex building that contains a sauna and gear storage room. The high, vaulted ceilings form a kind of canopy that connects the four parts of the house and makes them visually more spacious. The pine plywood, treated with lye and white oil and covering all walls and ceilings, offers a warm and protective experience. Nearly all of the furniture is made from the same material for a homogenous look.

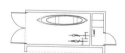

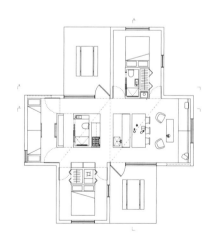

Architects: Rever & Drage Architects

Location: Molde, Norway
Completion: 2020
Gross floor area: 152 m²
Photography: Tom Auger

Zieglers Nest

Planning the house for this steep and relatively small plot, the architects also wished to use a limited amount of concrete for its foundation. They embraced the volume in variously articulated façades so that it gives the impression of consisting of four parts instead of one. Apart from the parking area, entrance, storage, and technical rooms on the ground floor, its innermost part opens up to a five-meter-high utility space for a trampoline and games. The rich plan includes a wardrobe, laundry room, and two bedrooms on the first level. The second floor, built as a log construction, has an impressive double height and serves as the common space with the kitchen, living room, and a library. The structurally connected top has one more bedroom, a bathroom, and a gallery with a balcony towards the main living space for family performances. The cherry on the cake is the roof terrace. Wood, mainly oak and pine, is used throughout the house to soften the dimensions and provide an intimate atmosphere.

This compact wooden structure was designed
to be tall and slim, with the ultimate goal of
a moderate footprint.

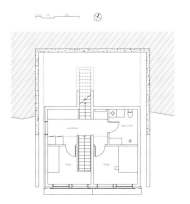

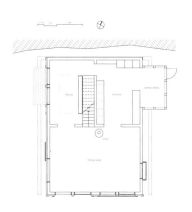

"This cabin in Ulvik, Western Norway, is a homage to country-road architecture," comment the architects, who draw from vernacular buildings, historical design principles, and traditional paintings.

Architect: Rever & Drage Architects

Location: Ulvik, Norway
Completion: 2020
Gross floor area: 142 m^2
Photography: Tom Auger

Cabin in Ulvik

The cabin draws from the composition of a traditional small-scale farm, as the architects explain. "Cabins as such, introduced to this area in the middle of the 20th century as recreation for the upper-middle class, were meant to function somewhere between the comfort of a house, and the roughness of a barn", the studio adds. Typical elements like the pitched roof, characteristic of both houses and barns, are juxtaposed with modern solutions like the large glazed parts of the walls, blurring the border between the landscape and the interiors. These windows are significantly sized, as the main façade faces a scenic fjord. Another elegant accent is the concrete arch inside the glass entrance, which also visually balances the slanted beam outside (the wooden beam is also functional, as it holds the drainage pipe from the roof). The cabin is made of very thick walls to protect the inhabitants from strong winds and rains, typical weather conditions in the region.

Architects: Erling Berg

Location: Norway
Completion: 2021
Gross floor area: 145 m²
Photography: Alejandro Villanueva

Kvitfjell Cabin

The all-present wood makes this cabin a snug, sheltered retreat, particularly in the winter, right in the middle of the amazing natural scenery.

Kvitfjell means "White Mountain" in Norwegian. On top of the mountain, as a discreet observation point, this narrow cabin was planned to embrace the views of neighboring mountain ranges. The architect, Erling Berg, decided to draw from traditional construction methods as well as traditional material – the house is built of pine wood that was sourced locally. The 26-meter-long timber volume is delightful. The outer shell – both the walls and roof – is made of untreated wood panels that will grey naturally over time. The exposed structure creates a three-dimensional effect on the façades and is only interrupted with simple glazings. The interiors are also entirely wrapped in wood, only here the surfaces are perfectly smooth and in white oiled pine, in order to make all the rooms brighter. While the common living space with a kitchen and a spacious dining area are open, they also follow the topography of the plot to frame the views, while the bedrooms are planned to offer maximum privacy on the opposite side.

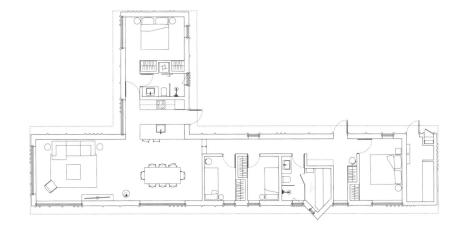

ERLING
BERG

Architects: Sjöblom Freij Arkitekter

Location: Kullavik, Sweden
Completion: 2022
Gross floor area: 190 m² + 55 m² conservatory
Photography: Sjöblom Freij Arkitekter

Kyvik House

The exterior shell, executed in untreated local heart pine, is intended to weather over time to blend the house in with the surrounding nature.

Made of three parts – the two-storey house, a heated conservatory, and a framed garden – Kyvik House creates a complex combination of forms. The architects play with the juxtaposition between the compact volume of the residential part and the other elements that are more lightweight and transparent to counterbalance their significant size. While the exposed wooden structure creates a consistent frame for all volumes, the programme was carefully planned based on the functions of each space, as well as the changing light conditions across various seasons. The exposed, load-bearing timber structure inside contributes to the distinctive atmosphere and highlights the tactile quality of the wood. The two levels are designed in a clear way – the lower is dedicated to social spaces, including a gallery-like living room as well as the parents' bedroom, and the original space of the conservatory. Accessible from the living room, it is entirely glazed and heated with a central burning stove that functions as a spacious extension, useful for different occasions.

Architects: Austigard Arkitektur

Location: Stavanger, Norway
Completion: 2019
Gross floor area: 90 m^2
Photography: Sindre Ellingsen

ABC Street House

Skilfully utilizing the narrow plot, the architects envisioned a shifted cube that is perfectly tuned with the surrounding low-scale architecture in an area promoting efficient energy consumption and a car-free lifestyle. The house is, quite visibly, divided into three vertical parts. The ground floor functions as an entrance and utilitarian space, the middle is occupied by the living area, and the top level, with views over the rooftops, offers a bright and spacious kitchen. The architects achieved an interesting contrast between the intimacy of the cave-like living room and the kitchen with ample daylight and access to an extensive rooftop terrace. The stairs connecting all parts were designed to create spatial continuity from the street level up to the roof level. As is typical for the local architecture, wood was used for the structure, but also for the indoor and outdoor cladding, which is made of birch and pine wood. The natural flooring throughout the house is in white oak.

The dynamically arranged volumes create a compact modern townhouse filling an empty lot in the dense urban fabric of Stavanger on the Norwegian coast.

Architects: Olsson Lyckefors Arkitektur

Location: Gothenburg, Sweden
Completion: 2019
Gross floor area: 285 m^2
Photography: Erik Lefvander

Villa Hovås

As the architects emphasize, Villa Hovås was envisaged to create the experience of "living in the view" without limiting the owners' privacy.

A striking view was the starting point for the design of the villa, located on sloping terrain facing the sealine and based on two contrasting plan layouts with a distinctive play of volumes. Its elongated shape is composed of the mostly solid street side and an entirely glazed façade directed toward the sea. "The sculpted volume and precise placement of openings create a variety and richness in the relationship to daylight and the surrounding nature," reflect the architects. The enveloping shell, made of black wooden slats, additionally filters the natural light. The high-light of the interiors, across two generously sized floors, is a spectacular living room spanning both levels with a massive glass wall opening it to the landscape. A large outdoor terrace and swimming pool extend this common area significantly on sunny days. The kitchen as well as the bedrooms are located on the top floor, allowing the inhabitants to benefit from panoramic vistas of the sea.

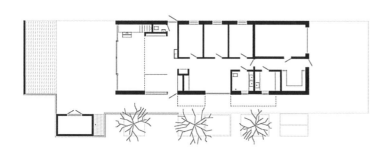

Architect: Johan Sundberg Arkitektur

Location: Skäne, Sweden
Completion: 2019
Gross floor area: 375 m²
Photography: Markus Linderoth

Villa MSV

While the entrance welcomes the residents with a bright brick façade, the opposite side of the house facing the garden is made entirely of wood, interrupted by numerous windows that fuse the interiors with the spacious outdoor area. The volume has been arranged to embrace three parts of the garden and to give them each a different function. A patio connected to the kitchen and living room is located toward the east and the rising sun. Toward the west, there is a special area for sitting, socialising, and dining. Finally, a long narrow pool is an extension of the sauna, bathing, and relaxation area in the southern wing of the house. To put the whole focus on the surrounding environment, which the large openings invite inside, filling all rooms with natural light, the interior design is devoid of superfluous elements. The limited range of colors and materials, as well as the wooden furniture, creates a perfect setting for a comfortable and relaxing habitat.

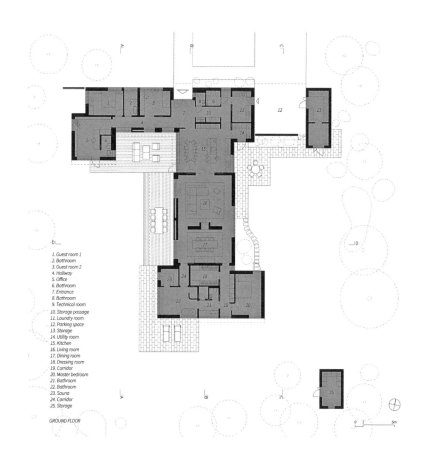

1. Guest room 1
2. Bathroom
3. Guest room 2
4. Hallway
5. Office
6. Bathroom
7. Entrance
8. Bathroom
9. Technical room
10. Storage passage
11. Laundry room
12. Parking space
13. Storage
14. Utility room
15. Kitchen
16. Living room
17. Dining room
18. Dressing room
19. Corridor
20. Master bedroom
21. Bathroom
22. Bathroom
23. Sauna
24. Corridor
25. Storage

GROUND FLOOR

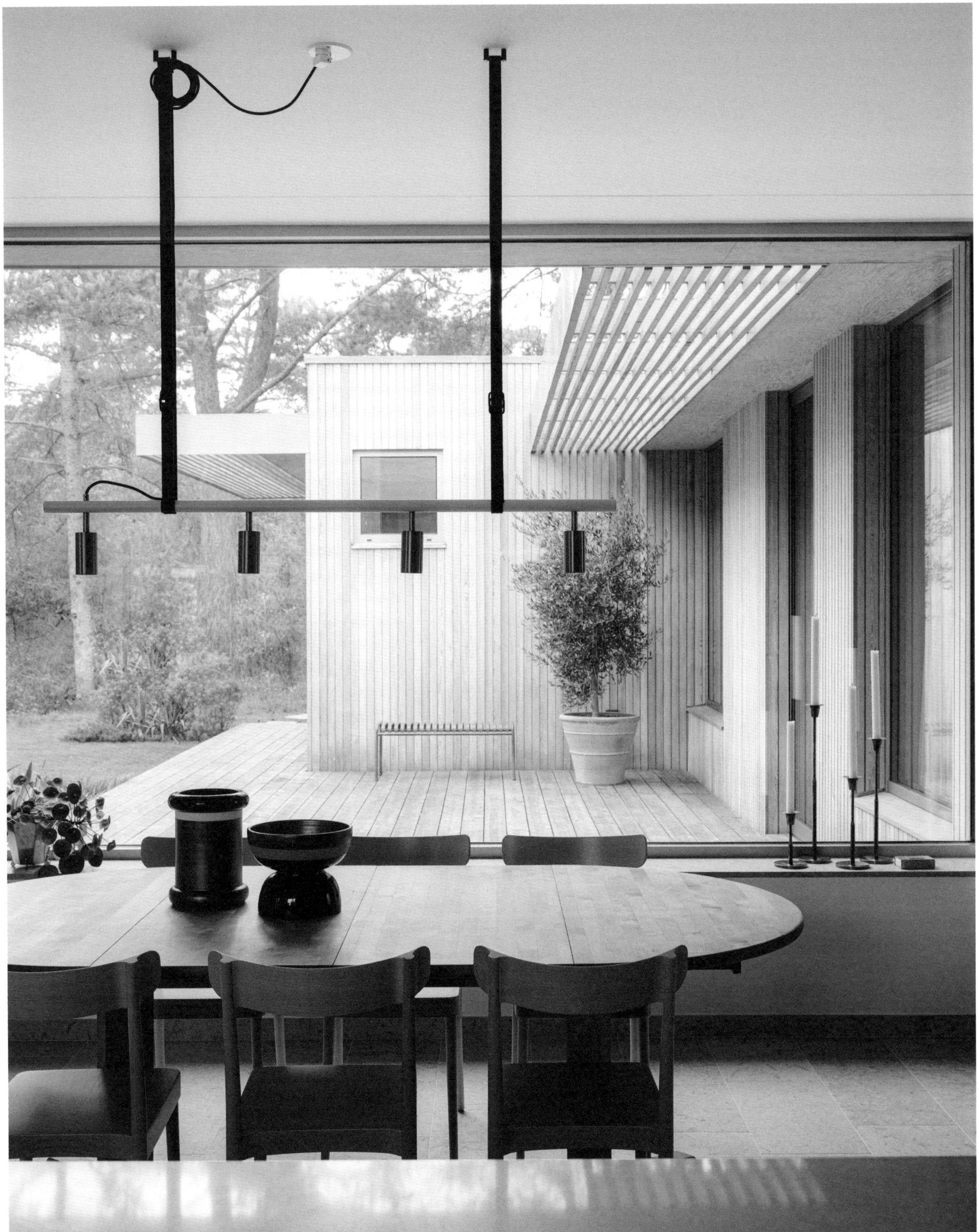

A quiet pine forest close to the white beaches of Ljunghusen became a home for this one-storey house for a multi-generational family.

"The starting-point has been
to create a generous house
in close contact with nature
in all directions, with grand
spaces inside but giving
a humble impression from
the outside," remarks the studio.

Architect: Johan Sundberg Arkitektur

Location: Ljunghusen, Sweden
Completion: 2018
Gross floor area: 241,5 m^2
Photography: Markus Linderoth

Summerhouse T

Another hide-out designed by Johan Sundberg Arkitektur in the middle of the forest, Summerhouse T is a distinctive retreat sitting on top of an island-like wooden terrace. Enveloping all façades of the complex yet low structure (a construction perfect for the local sandy terrain), the terrace creates a connection with the outdoors for every room in the house. Inhabitants can open one of numerous sliding glass doors and enjoy the fresh air and direct contact with nature. Additionally, the terrace is partly sheltered by the eaves of the gently sloping hip roof that covers the three-volume shape of the house. This solution provides shade and was meant to create a low visual expression with extended horizontal lines. Although it includes a few steel elements, the summer residence's framework is made of wood, with natural larch and dark stained fir used for its exterior walls. Wood is also present in the interiors, which are arranged comfortably and without superfluity.

Architect: Note Design Studio

Location: Stockholm, Sweden
Completion: 2017
Gross floor area: 200 m^2
Photography: Note Design Studio

Hidden
Tints

This carefully planned historical renovation gives old traits
a contemporary twist and an expressive color palette drawing
from original hues.

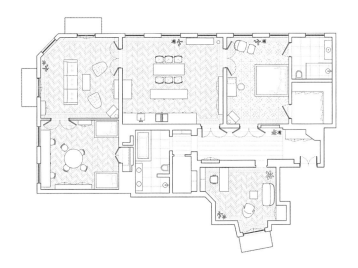

Previously the head office of a fashion brand in the heart of Stockholm, this extensive apartment located in a 19th-century tenement house was renovated to celebrate all elements of the historical architecture. The original wooden floors, stucco ornaments, and carpentry, as well as three old, tiled ovens were restored and preserved to create a special atmosphere. The space also required a new element, however: Note Design Studio decided to place some cabinets hovering on the walls and to keep others free-standing on the floor, to intervene in the most sensible way. The new color palette is based on the original colors found on original elements, including the tiled ovens inspiring the use of green, pink, and a yellowish white. "We added tones to the original color scale, which worked as a bridge between the powerful original hues, finally ending up with an 8-tone palette that originated from the hidden traces of the old apartment," the architects explain. The result is truly striking.

Architects: Atelier Tobia Zambotti

Location: Reykjavik, Iceland
Completion: 2020
Gross floor area: 40 m^2
Photography: Patrik Ontkovic

Gummi's 40sqm apartment

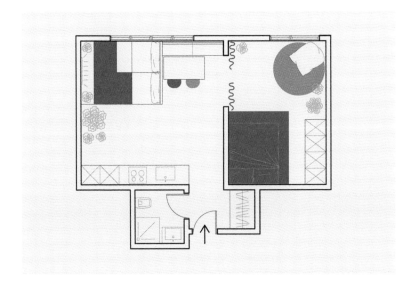

Envisioned as a minimalist-pop apartment and unconventional oasis in Iceland's capital, this two-room flat juxtaposes clear lines and quiet tones with distinctive accents of color. A candy-like pink and electric blue are used only on selected elements, like the painter's brush pattern on the wall of the living and dining area. Some sophisticated solutions enhancing the interior also have a functional task, like the ceiling with a geometric pattern made of foam typically used in recording studios, that supports the acoustics. Others, like the electric blue curtain dividing the day and night spaces, are used in a decorative, nearly theatrical way. Some lively additions to the space are several lush green plants, creating distinctive spots in both rooms. The Italian bespoke furniture, custom-made by Falegnameria Caldini Luca, and also referring to the original color palette, is a perfect fit for this futuristic interior. Minimalism with extravagant touches challenges the traditional Nordic style, infusing it with more color and playfulness.

Tobia Zambotti designs Nordic-style living with original flair, where spartan meets with eccentric, all adjusted to a very compact space.

One of the oldest residential areas in Frederiksberg, Denmark, becomes a home to this partly hidden villa, where tradition meets modernity.

Architect: EFFEKT Architects

Location: Frederiksberg, Denmark
Completion: 2019
Gross floor area: 200 m^2
Photography: EFFEKT / Kristian Holm

Villa Bülowsvej

An urban villa for a family with three children, Bülowsvej takes an L-shape, defined by its distinctive pitch roof. The architects adjusted the design both to the historical neighbouring houses from the 1800s and to preserve a centenary beech tree on the plot. Their solution is a classical and relatively spacious volume (the expansive ground floor is topped only with the level hidden under the sloping roof). Maximizing the floor plan through the use of clean straight lines as well as symmetry principles was the main objective. The outer shell of the villa is made of black-stained cedar wood lamellae that seamlessly integrate the window frames and solar panels. Numerous openings, including the double-height full-width glass façade, allowed the architects to create a great sense of space inside. The bright palette of colors in the interiors is warmly accompanied by wooden furnishings. The quintessentially Nordic aesthetics are highlighted by the ample natural light.

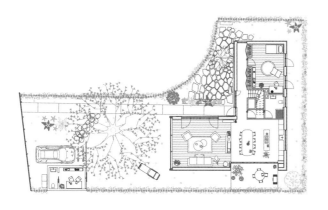

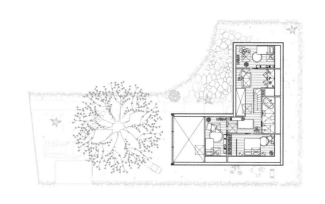

Architects: Pushak

Location: Kirkøy, Hvaler, Norway
Completion: 2020
Gross floor area: 90 m²
Photography: Ivan Brodey

Hytte Hvaler

Located at the edge of a forest overlooking the coastline, Cabin Hvaler, with rocks and pines forming its adjacent garden, is a discreet addition to the scenery.

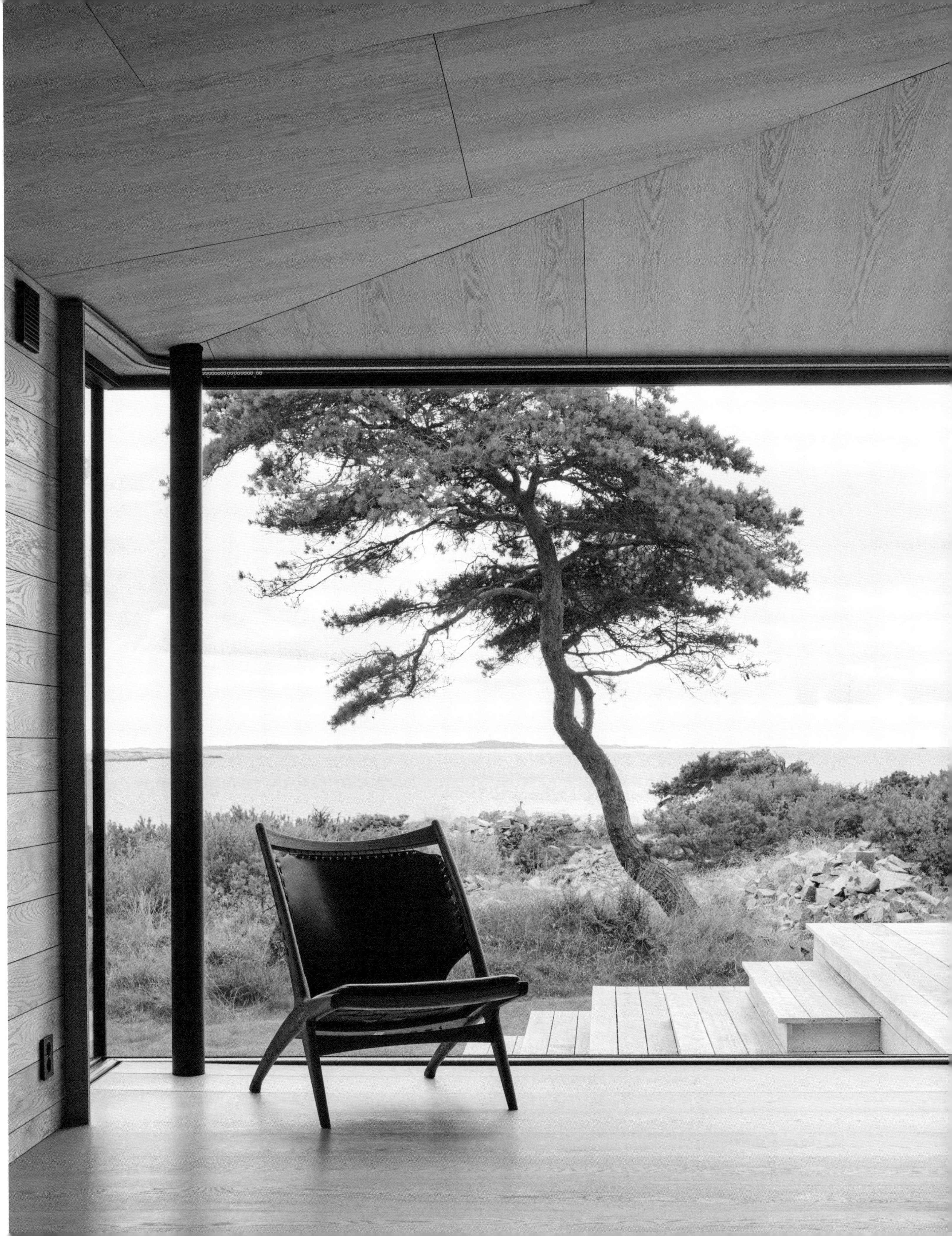

While replacing a former cabin on the plot, the architects had one main objective – to minimize their interference with the native landscape. Constructed exactly on the same footprint, the new house becomes invisible within the surrounding natural context. It has effective protection from the wind and the rain, which is well-drained through the asymmetrical shape of the roof. The materials selected for the roof and walls, textured brick, work both for the weather conditions and to create a camouflage effect. The idea was to design a compact square volume, which placed on a flat concrete foundation would look as if it were floating above the landscape. The kitchen together with the living room are unquestionably the main focus of the plan. Located to the south, this space can be extended outside towards the terrace with a sea view through the windows, opening to the full width of the house. Four bedrooms and two bathrooms complete the cozy programme. The interiors are softly embraced by a solid oak floor, and oak paneling on the walls and plywood ceilings.

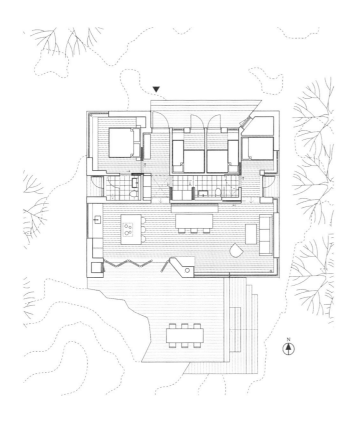

Architects: DELIN Arkitektkontor

Location: Älgö, Sweden
Completion: 2019
Gross floor area: 245 m²
Photography: Karin Bergquist (exterior),
Louise Bilgert (interiors)

Shutter House

The architect, inspired by the hilly location surrounded by a young settlement, aimed to design a residence that would be unique in style. Carefully planned details and integration with the plot were at the heart of the concept. The two floors are visually clearly divided. The ground level was envisioned as the public part, with an entrance and toilet, as well as the kitchen and living room, joined through a specially built fireplace that faces both directions. The living area received a direct connection with the garden and in the future, it will also be extended through a Japanese garden. The top floor offers more social areas, as well as three bedrooms, a bathroom, and a small writing den in the loft. With the over four-meter-high ceiling and one entirely glazed façade, this space has a completely different atmosphere. "The house feels dynamic as you move inside it, as light and seasons are always present. It's a house that offers many changing perspectives and impressions throughout the year." remarks the architect.

This ingeniously shaped house is defined by sharp lines
and spacious volumes, where geometry is enhanced
by light and the atmospheric combination of natural
wood and concrete.

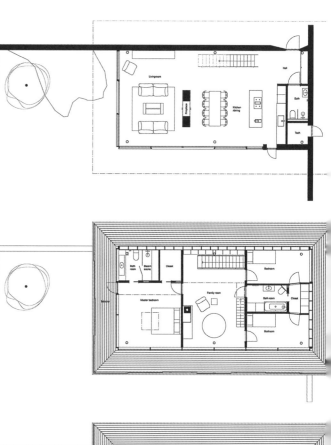

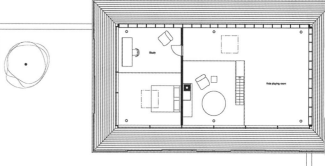

Architects: Studio Bua

Location: Skarðsströnd, Iceland
Completion: 2021
Gross floor area: 182 m^2
Photography: Marino Thorlacius

Hlöðuberg
Artist's Studio

This stunning transformation of a former concrete barn in a rural Icelandic landscape has resulted in a thoughtful combination of a house and an artist's studio.

The artist's studio, kitchen, and dining space occupy the ground floor, while the domestic sphere, including the private areas, takes the top level, to find the right balance between creative and family life. The plan accommodates a double-height space at each end, one of which is the workspace. The interiors, envisioned in a pared down aesthetic to minimize clutter, are kept neutral through calm hues and the omnipresence of plywood, ensuring that they don't distract from the artwork on display. They also contrast starkly with the wild surroundings, seen from many openings framing beautifully the views of the expansive landscape in various directions. To preserve the barn's unique character, the architects wished to keep as much of the existing structure as possible. It was stabilized and a lightweight, two-storey timber structure was inserted. To withstand the harsh weather conditions on site (the plot is surrounded by mountains, meadows, a fjord, and the sea), this new volume is clad in resistant corrugated industrial Aluzinc, produced locally.

List of architects

Avanto Architects (46-55)

avan.to

Atelier Oslo (76-85)

atelieroslo.no

Atelier Tobia Zambotti (200-203)

tobiazambotti.com

Austigard Arkitektur (174-177)

austigard.no

C.F. Møller Architects (18-27)

cfmoller.com

DELIN Arkitektkontor (212-217)

delinarkitektkontor.se

EFFEKT Architects (204-207)

effekt.dk

Erling Berg (164-169)

erlingberg.com

Feste Landscape • Architecture (72-75)

feste.no

Force4 Architects (28-31)

force4.dk

Ida Katrine Friis Tinning (102-107)

idatinning.com

Johan Sundberg Arkitektur (184-193)

johansundberg.com

Kvalbein Korsøen Arkitektur (86-91)

kvalbeinarkitektur.no

Lie Øyen arkitekter (130-133)

lieoyen.no

Marge Arkitekter (96-101)

marge.se

Mork-Ulnes Architects (142-153)

morkulnes.com

N+P ARKITEKTUR (114-121)

nplusp.dk

Norm Architects (12-17)

normcph.com

NORRØN Architects (8-11)

norroen.dk

Note Design Studio (194-199)

notedesignstudio.se

Olsson Lyckefors Arkitektur (178-183)

olssonlyckefors.se

PAVE Architects (38-41)

pavearkkitehdit.fi

Pirinen & Salo Oy (66-71)

pirinensalo.com

Pushak (208-211)

pushak.no

R21 Arkitekter (134-141)

r21.no

Rever & Drage Architects (154-163)

reverdrage.no

Sanden+Hodnekvam Architects (61-65, 92-95)

sandenhodnekvam.no

Seppo Mäntylä (42-45)

seppomantyla.fi

Sigurd Larsen Design & Architecture (32-37)

sigurdlarsen.com

Sjöblom Freij Arkitekter (170-173)

sjoblomfreij.se

Studio Bua (218-221)

studiobua.com

Studio David Thulstrup (122-129)

studiodavidthulstrup.com

Studio Holmberg (108-113)

studioholmberg.se

Studio Puisto (56-59)

studiopuisto.fi

The Deutsche Nationalbibliothek lists this publication in the Deutsche
Nationalbibliografie; detailed bibliographic data are available on
the Internet at http://dnb.dnb.de

ISBN 978-3-03768-285-2
© 2023 by Braun Publishing AG
www.braun-publishing.ch

1st edition 2023
Text, layout, cover design: © Agata Toromanoff / Fancy Books Packaging UG
Copy-editing: Allison Silver Adelman
Graphic concept: Martin Decker
Reproduction: Bild1Druck GmbH, Berlin

Front cover photo: © Ivar Kvaal
Backcover photos: top left © Hans Koistinen; top right © Note Design Studio;
bottom © Ivan Brodey